Daily Meditations

for

Better Living

Empowering you through God's Word

Daily Meditations

for

Better Living

Empowering you through God's Word

Missionary Verna C. Starks

ISBN-13: 978-1535108454
ISBN-10: 1535108452

Bible references taken from *American King James (*entered into the public domain on November 8, 1999); *The Holy Bible*, New King James Version, Copyright © 1982 by Thomas Nelson, Inc.; and *Holy Bible*, New International Version®, NIV® Copyright © 1973, 1978, 1984, 2011 by Biblica, Inc.®, Used by permission.

For information on the content of this publication, please contact Verna Starks, vstarks18@att.net.

Published by WrightStufco

803-446-6096
www.wrightstuf.com

Printed in the United States of America

DEDICATION

This book is dedicated to my wonderful and loving children: Elmer Lorance, William, Jr., and Charnice Esther, my first teachers, my parents, Deacon Lawrence and Deaconess Esther Henderson Chaplin, my dear sisters Azalee Chaplin Bishop and Edith Chaplin Patterson (deceased), my two brothers, Johnnie L. and Lawrence Chaplin, Jr. (deceased). To my wonderful nephews and nieces: Angela, Robin, Ricky, Aaron, Bert, Carlton, Lawrence Chaplin III, Christopher, and Brandon. To my god-daughter, the late Angela M. Johnson, and to all my church and neighborhood mothers and sisters in Christ for their teachings, love and compassion to mold my life for the journey.

Dedicated to Dreamers: as I look at my life through God's eyes, I see more clearly the blessings God has bestowed upon me, my children, and grandchildren's lives. I say thank you Lord for the valleys and mountains you brought me through. "For every tree is known by his own fruit" (Luke 6:44). As you read the daily meditations, I encourage you to invest in your dream, God is no respecter of persons (Acts 10:34). A person's gift will make room for him and bring him before great men....Proverbs 18:16. Let the church say Amen

ACKNOWLEDGEMENTS

With unconditional love and special thanks to my two sons and one daughter: the eldest son, Elmer Lorance (Yolanda) Starks, who leads the family with love and a sense of humor. When you were tasked with leading the family, you followed God's word found in Psalm 37:23, "The steps of a good man are ordered by the Lord and He delights in your ways." I am very proud of you and your commitment to your family, church, and friends. **You are a true champion in the family**.

To William Edward "Billy" (Julanda) Starks, Jr., my youngest son, you are loving and gentle. I thank you for your faithfulness to the family and church. "God will not forget your work and labor of love which you have shown over and over again. Hebrews 6:10." Your gentleness is a virtue, I thank you for your telephone call each morning to check in, and I really enjoy our weekly visits. Commit your ways unto the Lord and serve Him with all your heart, mind, and soul. **You are a blue ribbon son**. To my daughter, Dr. Charnice Esther Starks (Tyson, Sr.) Ray, thank you for your continued love to our family and extended family. You were born on Father's Day morning, the family and neighbors have cheered for you from Day 1. Thank you for our daily conversations as we encourage each other. You are a Proverbs 31 Woman. "Give her of the fruit of her hands and let her own works praise her in the gates." I witness your awesome walk with the Lord as you completed your Doctor of Education degree in 2015, while managing the family, job, church, and friendships. Thank you for the many lives you impact each day. **Your inner strength, beauty and anointing will last a lifetime.** During the death of daddy Starks, each one of you showed strength, yet leaned on each other, I thank God for your professionalism and his final wishes were followed.

To my adorable and precious grandchildren: Satori, Jasmine, Scottie, Tiffani-Shae, Tyler, Tyson, Jr., and Parker, you are so special to grandma. I pray (Jeremiah 29:11), promise over your life, you will be blessed and be a blessing to others (Proverbs 11:25). To my faithful prayer partners, the 100+ daily readers, and Sisters Pamela Mills and Bennette Johnson whose encouragement helped me through this project, I thank you. To all my goddaughters: Mrs. Tawanda Webb and Ms. Niovia Davis, my god sisters Dr. Tricia Witherspoon and Ms. Peggy Harrison, I love you and will cherish your friendship forever. Thank you to my pastor, Reverend Dr. Derrick Scott for giving me your blessing and praying for me.

To my sanctuary mothers, Mrs. Pauline B. Richardson, the late Mrs. Telicious L. Kenly Boyd and sponsors, thank you for investing in my future and sending me on a trip to the *Motherland: Senegal and Gambia, South Africa,* this trip impacted my life to be a better servant to humanity. To all the names that I answer to: "Mommy, MaMa, Grandma, Mother Starks, Ms. Verna, Sister Verna, and friend, I love you." To my Internet Ministry partners who shared stories, struggles, joys, longings and desires, God is faithful to His word. To Sister Toretha Wright, editor and long-time sister in Christ, you are special and your encouragement for this book has been awesome.

Love,
Mother Starks

THE MEDITATIONS

PREFACE

To God be the Glory – what a joy to see this God given vision come to pass. Godly reverence and humility are hallmarks of my life because I'm yielded to the Holy Spirit. I believe in the power of prayer and studying God's word.

This book will address 40 Daily Meditations that will EMPOWER your everyday living. The ideas in each meditation are powerful reminders of God's love, commandments, and His promises to His children.

A member of St. Paul African Methodist Episcopal Church, I have been a Licensed Missionary since 2004. In July, 2011, my family was in Orlando, Florida to attend the Connectional Women's Missionary Society and Young People Division Quadrennial of the African Methodist Episcopal Church. While I enjoyed the meetings each day, this particular morning I remained in the hotel and spent some time worshipping and praying to God. I was retired and needed to hear from the Master about my future. God whispered softly –what do you have to give me? I answered the Lord! I had just purchased a new computer before our trip. He said, begin an Internet Ministry with your life's experience through a daily word to strengthen, EMPOWER and encourage others.

As I reflect on my life, I am so thankful to God for my wonderful parents, my three wonderful children, seven grandchildren, one sibling, and cousins. As the middle child of five, my mother would allow me to visit my grandmother seven days a week. My grandmother would sit with me and teach me how to write letters to her daughters who lived in Detroit, Michigan and Bayonne, New Jersey. My Aunt Pearl Brown called me **the *love child*.**

My family has been long time Baptist for four generations. After graduation from high school, my family assumed that I would attend an in-state Baptist School. I was also the child who wanted to take risks in life. I enrolled and graduated from Lincoln Business College, Jacksonville, Florida and later graduated from a Baptist College, Morris College, Sumter, South Carolina with a degree in Ministerial Studies. I've attended Lutheran Seminary for special courses to prepare me for a lifetime of serving others.

I learned the power of prayer and the commitment to pray from my mother. My mother was always ordering books on meditations and prayer. Truly, her light is brightly shining as I complete this season in my life.

To all my Internet Ministry family, from the following pages, may you find comfort, faith, strength, trust, hope, and expectation as you unlock faith's power in your life. God's word is pure, full of wisdom to EMPOWER you for better living, even when unwanted circumstances visit, your soul will be anchored in the Lord.

Daily Meditations

ATTITUDE

"Set your mind on the things above, not on the things that are on earth."
~1 Colossians 3:2

MEDITATION

The longer I live, the more I realize the impact of my ATTITUDE. Our ATTITUDE is 90% of how we view life's circumstances. I am learning the great lesson found in the Book of Ecclesiastes:

There is a time to speak and a time to be silent.

I am learning not to judge others on my small thinking ability, and I thank God for giving me this revelation.

Christians have hurt others by the comments they have made, and relationships have been broken by this small senseless act. As you begin your day "set your mind on things above, not on the things that are on earth."

Learn not to respond so quickly to every situation, meditate and trust God, I believe the home and church will become Christ-focus and we will make a difference in the world around us.

PRAYER

Dear Father, forgive me for hurting others with my attitude. Thank You for reminding me that You are the judge. Help me to be more loving and kind when interacting with others, and to trust You in every circumstance. Thank You for loving us and sending Your Son to this world to save us from our sins. In Jesus' name. Amen.

OPTIMISM!

"I can do all things through Christ who strengthens me."
~Philippians.4:13

MEDITATION

As believers, we have every reason to think optimistically. Begin today, and at least several times each day, affirm this thought: I expect the best and with God leading and guiding me, I will attain the best. "The Lord is patient with you, not wanting anyone to perish, but everyone to come to repentance 1 Peter 2:9 says," But ye are a chosen generation, a royal priesthood, an holy nation, a peculiar people; that ye should shew forth the praises of him who hath called you out of darkness into his marvelous light." Think optimistically!

PRAYER

Dear Lord, let me be an expectant believer. Let me expect the best from You each day, and let me look for the best in others each day. Lord, my ways are not Your ways, for Your thoughts and ways are higher than mine. I will look unto You from whence comes all my help. Thank You Lord for giving me Your best. In Jesus' name. Amen.

BLESSINGS OF PEACE

"The God of PEACE be with you all."
~Romans 15:33

MEDITATION

The Father sent His Son, Jesus into the world to save us from our sins. His name shall be called: Wonderful, Counselor, The Mighty God, The everlasting Father, The Prince of Peace (Isaiah 9:6). Peace is full confidence that God is Who He says He is and that He will keep every promise in His word. John 14:27 gives us hope: Jesus offers us peace, not as the world gives, but as He alone gives. Be ye transformed by the renewing of your mind and you will find unending peace. Ask Jesus to help you share His peace and the message of the cross to those who are perishing. His peace will empower your life.

PRAYER

Dear Lord, when I turn my thoughts and prayers to You, I feel the peace that You intend for my life. When I become distracted by the busyness of the day or the demands of the moment, whisper to me to trust You and lean on You and follow Your commands and accept Your peace. In Jesus Name. Amen

PRAISE

"Declare His glory among the nations, His wonders among all peoples."
~ Psalm 96:3

MEDITATION

There is a song that I like by William Murphy entitled, *Praise Is What I Do.* (Praise is what I do, when I want to be close to You... Jesus). Today, as I write to you, I have a dear friend of 40 years who had open-heart surgery on November 3. Since that time, she has been back to surgery three times. I just begin to PRAISE God this morning and encourage myself and trust God. The psalmist reminds us, we have the high and holy privilege to declaring, "His glory among the nations, His wonders among all people." Praise God, after 3 months, my friends continues to get stronger each day, her strength has been a blessing to me, when I become discouraged, I will praise the Lord.

PRAYER

Dear Lord, I thank You for my family and friends. I lift them up to You today in PRAISE. Give us grace for the journey, and bless those who care for our love ones. We thank You for Your healing power physically, emotionally, and spiritually. Blessed are those whose trust is in the Lord. This we ask In Jesus' name. Amen

Special note: Attend church on Sunday and celebrate daily with PRAISE to our loving Savior!

TAKING REFUGE

"The name of the Lord is a strong tower, the
righteous run to it and are safe."
~ Proverbs 18: 1

MEDITATION

As believers in Christ Jesus, we can take refuge in Him
each day. The name of Jesus is a strong tower and
believers run to it and are safe. The word safe means
set on high and out of danger. Each morning, seek God
and run to Him for guidance and in the evening, it is
good so say "Thank you Lord" for keeping me from seen
an unseen dangers. The name of the Lord is a strong
tower, the righteous run to it and are safe. Our God is a
Promise Keeper!

PRAYER

Dear Lord, the world is in turmoil, but I thank You that I can run to You and feel secure. I thank You that I can trust You early in the morning and late at night. Hallelujah to Your Name! Amen.

ASKING GOD

"But my God shall supply all your need according to His riches in glory by Jesus Christ." ~Philippians 4:19

MEDITATION

God sent His only begotten Son to Calvary's cross to save us from our sins. What are you in need of today? Are you heavy laden and burden from your pass? Do you desire a new beginning in your life? Ask God to sustain you, take your worries to Him in prayer. Seek God's strength and direction for your life and those of which you are responsible for making decisions. Trust God and obey His will according to His Holy Word. He is waiting to bless you and take care of your need according to His riches in glory by Jesus Christ. God is a Promise Keeper. You can trust and depend on Him - Hallelujah to His Name.

PRAYER

Dear God, help me to serve You only. Lord, when I become discouraged, let me turn to You. When I am weak, let me seek strength from You. When I am fearful, keep my mind stayed on You and Your love for me. In all things, forgive me for my sins. Today is a new beginning in my life. I accept Your will and Your way. In Jesus' name. Amen.

BLESSINGS

"For thou Lord, will bless the righteous."
~ Psalm 5:12

MEDITATION

God gives us so many blessings that they are too numerous to count. To name a few blessings, our life, family, health, freedom, friends and talents. But the greatest blessing to humanity is God's Son, Jesus, who came to give all who believe in Him - SALVATION. We give thanks to God for blessing us each day. It is our duty to tell the good news of Jesus' saving grace to others.

PRAYER

Dear Lord, thank You for Your many blessings. May I live each day with thanksgiving in my heart and praise on my lips. Thank You for the gift of health, family, friends, and extended family. Thank You for the promise of eternal life. May my life impact those who are waiting to hear the Good News of Jesus. In Jesus' name Amen

THE BIBLE

"Thy word is a lamp unto our feet, and a light unto my path."
~ Psalm 119:105

MEDITATION

God has given us the Holy Bible so that we might know His commandments, His wisdom, His love, and His Son. Psalm 119: 105 is our guide for our family, friends, and others whom God will send in our paths. Learn to apply His Word to your daily life. He is a rewarder to those who diligently seek Him. Let the church say Amen!

PRAYER

Dear Father, the Bible is Your gift to me; let me use it and share it with my family. When I stray from Your Holy Word Lord, remind me of the power of Your Word. Help me to be a faithful student of Your Word. In Jesus' name. Amen.

CHARACTER

"In everything set them an example by doing what is good."
~ Titus 2:7

MEDITATION

Our character is built slowly over a lifetime. Jesus' character was so impeccable, so noble, so honest, so compassionate, and so loving, to name a few, that many followed Him on His journey. Our character is so precious and should be built on truth, honesty, compassion, and love. Character is difficult to build but easy to tear down. Value your character, others are watching you. If you are a parent, you are your child's first teacher. Our character is made in small moments every day of our lives. What character are you displaying? Would anyone be willing to follow your leadership at home, in the community, at church or the workplace? VALUE YOUR CHARACTER, it will take you places that God has prepared just for you. Amen

PRAYER

Dear Father, let me be a person of honesty, truth, love, and compassionate. May I be Your worthy servant and may I live according to Your commandments. Lord, help me to live godly before my children, grandchildren, and others. Lord, I thank You for Your love for my family, my friends, and me. May my life be a testimony to You and others. In Jesus' name. Amen

DISCIPLINE

"He who heeds discipline shows the way to life, but whoever ignores correction leads others astray."
~ Proverbs 10:17

MEDITATION

Believers who study the Bible are transformed by the renewing of your mind. God intends that we lead DISCIPLINE lives. God does not reward half-truths, laziness, or misbehavior. These behaviors may be entertaining, but are contrary to God's will. If you are lacking in any area of your life, pray to your Father in heaven and ask Him to give you a thirst for His Word. God expects believers to adopt a DISCIPLINED approach to their lives. We must teach the next generation the word of God and by living a life that pleases Him. The day is far spent and night is upon us. It's imperative that the home and church return to the sure foundation - Jesus Christ. He is the same yesterday, today, and forever. Today, begin to live for Jesus!

PRAYER

Dear Lord, let me begin today to live a life that pleases You. Forgive me for my selfish behavior and disobedience. Lord, I want to be faithful to You. Help me to follow Your commandments and teach others Your way. Lord, let me be faithful in following You. In Jesus' name. Amen.

GRATITUDE

"In all your ways acknowledge Him, and He will make your paths straight."
~ Proverbs 3:6

MEDITATION

As we grow older, being grateful should become a lifestyle. I am grateful to God for sending His only Son, Jesus Christ to die for my sins. I am grateful to God for my family, health, employment and retirement, extended family, church family, and peace, to name a few. Take time daily to say thank you to God, and remember, He is the giver of all good things and rewarder to those who diligently seek Him. Hallelujah!

PRAYER

Dear Father, I want my attitude to be one of gratitude. You have given me so much. When I think of Your grace and Your goodness to me, I am humbled and thankful every day. May my life impact others for You. In Jesus' name. Amen

HOLY GHOST POWER

*"You shall receive POWER when the HOLY SPIRIT
comes upon you; and you shall be witnesses to me."*
~ Acts 1:8

MEDITATION

As followers of Christ, we are called to be witnesses of
what Jesus has done for us. We don't have to explain
every detail of the blessings, just be able to share the
"good news" of Jesus and His love for humanity. As we
rely on the Spirit's power, we can point a hurting world
to the redeeming Savior. The Holy Ghost Power will
allow you to be an effective witness and *go ye therefore
and teach all nations about the love of Jesus*, and His
saving grace. Let your testimony be your witness today!

PRAYER

Dear Lord, thank You for loving us and sending a Savior to redeem us from our sins. May I impact someone today with Your love. I thank You and I ask for boldness as I begin this new journey of sharing the good news of a loving Savior. In Jesus' name. Amen.

LOVING GOD

"We love Him, because He first loved us."
~ 1 John4:19

MEDITATION

The older I get, the more I believe our physical, and emotional health is exactly proportional to our love for God. If we enjoy the spiritual health that God intends for our lives, we must praise Him and love Him every day. If you find your schedule so packed with "a too do list" and you are running from place to place on a daily basis, seek God for guidance and wait for His instructions. Don't allow yourself to be pulled in every direction and miss spending time with the Father. After all, we love Him, because He first loved us.

PRAYER

Dear Father, You have blessed my family with a love that is eternal. May we spend time with You each day. Lord, may we show our love to You by sharing Your message of salvation to others. Lord, thank You for loving the world so much that You sent Your only Son to die for our sins. In Jesus' name. Amen.

SEEKING GOD

"But seek ye first the kingdom of God and His righteousness, and all things shall be added unto you."
~ Matthew 6~33

MEDITATION

Do you find yourself upset over the least little situation? Do you find yourself unhappy in your workplace, the church, and even your home? Seek God, He is waiting to hear from His children. God is everywhere you have ever been and everywhere you will ever go. He knows your every thought and He hears your every heartbeat. When you earnestly seek Him, you'll find Him because He has risen from the grave and He is Lord over all. Psalm 92: 1-2 reads: It's good to Seek Him each morning and praise Him every evening for blessing you and keeping you throughout the day. With every revelation that God is with you comes an invitation to adjust your busy schedule and spend time with Him each day! Seek Him and wait to hear from Him. His plans and ways are higher than yours.

PRAYER

Heavenly Father, forgive me for starting my day without seeking You first. Let me reach out to You and let me praise You for Your goodness and mercy in my life. As I seek You, I trust Your will and plans for my life. Thank You Lord. In Jesus' name. Amen.

SERVING OTHERS

"Be ye therefore merciful, as your Father also is merciful."
~Luke 6:36

MEDITATION

I praise God for my wonderful parents, especially my loving mother. She was full of love and believed in helping everybody! I have a plaque she gave me years ago that reads: *"Please be patient with others, God is still working things out in their lives too."*

In my golden years, this message has so much meaning. Serving others has been weaved in the fabric of my being. Paul's letter in the New Testament: Philippians 2:4 is a reminder: "Look not every man on his own things, but every man also on the things of others." As I witness my children and grandchildren, I am thankful to pass this life lesson to them. Those that are planted in the house of the Lord shall flourish in the courts of our God.   Serving others is truly a blessing.

PRAYER

Dear Father, enable me to respect and love others. Help me to be patient and never give up on those you send in my path. Help me to be nurturing, loving, and kind always. In Jesus' name. Amen.

YOUR GIFT

"Your gift will make room for you and bring you before righteous people."
~ Proverbs 18:16

MEDITATION

My mother shared the above scripture with me decades ago, and before she went to be with the Lord, she gave me a printed inscription that reads: *"Your gift will make room for you and bring you before righteous people."* According to Jeremiah 29:11, God has a plan and purpose for each one of His children. Renew your mind in the Word of God. Jesus' mission was to empower His disciples to perform miracles before going to the cross. Your gift is to glorify God and to love others as yourself. Your gift will make room for you and bring you to your next assignment. Stop fighting to stay at a place where you have completed your mission. Move in the direction God is leading you, His promises are sure and His ways and thoughts are higher than ours and His Word will not return unto Him void. Jesus Is a Promise Keeper - Hallelujah!

PRAYER

Dear Lord, thank You for sending Your beloved Son, Jesus Christ to save us from sin and empower us for our mission. Help me to study Your Word and renew my mind that I may be a blessing to my family, friends, and others that You send in my path. Lord, I need You every hour, every hour I need You. Oh bless me now my Savior, I come to thee. In Jesus' name. Amen.

RENEWAL

"I will give you a new heart and put a new spirit in you."
~ Ezekiel 36:26

MEDITATION

As believers, God intends that His children lead joyous lives filled with abundance, love, and peace. Turn your heart to God in prayer for **renewal** and **restoration**. Make time to delve into God's Holy Word, attend Bible Study/ Church School, and worship as often as you can, and renew your vows with Him. When you do, you'll discover that the Creator of the universe stands ready and able to give you a new heart and put a new spirit in you. He is a God of wholeness.

PRAYER

Dear Lord, sometimes I feel alone and sometimes I grow weary. Please give me strength each day to feel Your healing touch. Let me draw strength from Your promises and from Your unending love. Thank You Lord. In Jesus' name Amen.

Attend the Church of your choice and be blessed!

VISIBLE LIFE

Now then, we are ambassadors for Christ as though
God were pleading through us.
~ 2 Corinthians 5:20

MEDITATION

Believers are ambassadors for Christ on earth. How visible is your life for Christ? As a believer, when we show up in any given setting, others should see an aroma of loving people, Christian values, principles, and morals as a witness for Christ. Ask yourself - do others see Christ in my life? The scripture is clear. "Let everyone examine his/her life and see if you are in the faith." We are Ambassadors for Christ in the earth; there is a neighbor, coworker, and even a friend waiting to hear the Good News of Jesus' saving power. We are Christ's feet, hands, and mouthpiece. Now then, we are ambassadors for Christ as though God were pleading through us. Hallelujah!

PRAYER

Dear Lord, I thank You for Your saving grace in my life. Help me to re-dedicate my life to telling others the Good News of Your saving power. I need the Holy Spirit to dwell in my heart. Give me the compassion to love those who are hurting and have not heard Your gospel to be a witness to them. In Jesus' name. Amen.

ARE YOU EMPTY THIS SEASON?

*"He satisfies the longing soul, and fills the hungry
soul with goodness."*
~ Psalm 107:9

MEDITATION

If we are honest with ourselves, we all have empty
seasons sometime. The empty seasons include: lack of
love, losing friendship(s), loss of love ones and security.
If you are a believer, you are in covenant agreement
with God. Delight yourself in the Lord and He will give
you the desires of your heart. He is Our Eternal God
(our Creator), our Jehovah El Shaddai (our Supplier),
Jehovah-Jireh (our Provider), Jehovah Rapha (our
Healer), Jehovah-Nissi (our banner), Jehovah-Shalom
(our peace), Jehovah-Shammah (His Abiding
Presence). He can satisfy the EMPTY soul. If you find
yourself empty and complaining more than you are

thankful, your soul is longing for Jesus! Jesus alone fills the soul with good things all year long (Psalm 107:9). He is a Promise Keeper!

PRAYER

Dear Loving Father, fill me with Your goodness and love. Lord, without You, I have nothing and I feel empty. Thank You for the abiding satisfaction that I find in You. Forgive me for complaining instead of being thankful. In Jesus' name. Amen.

ANGER

*"A soft answer turns away wrath, but harsh words
stir up ANGER."*
~Proverbs: 15:1

MEDITATION

Everyone has experienced ANGER! Growing up with
two sisters and two brothers, we kept something stirred
up all time. As parents with two sons and one daughter
in our household, we witness the sibling ANGER. Oh,
how I thank God for loving parents who taught us to
love each other and always look out for each other. It
was constant in our home to provide and teach love to
our children. Through the sacrifice of Jesus' death and
resurrection, we are the benefactors of love instead of
ANGER. The next time ANGER arises in your heart,
whisper a prayer - and ANGER will flee from you.

PRAYER

Dear Lord, I thank You for reminding me to turn to You when I am angry. Let me be quick to forgive others and find love and peace from Your example. May my life impact others with love instead of anger. In Jesus' name. Amen.

GIVING ALL

"Thanks be to God for His indescribable gift."
~ 2 Corinthians 9:15

MEDITATION

Throughout the year, we share gifts with others. Everyday, take some time and meditate on the most precious gift given to us by our heavenly Father - His Son, Jesus Christ. Our Father demonstrated the ultimate sacrifice of GIVING ALL. No gift we give to others can be compared with the Savior. We thank God for the indescribable gift of Jesus. Share the good news of Jesus with someone.

PRAYER

Dear Father, we thank You for GIVING ALL for us. May we be ever mindful that we need to share the good news of Your Son with our family, neighbors, and others who cross our paths. We ask for the Holy Spirit to dwell in us, and make us bold in sharing Your gospel. We thank and love You. This we ask In Jesus' name. Amen

LOVE WITHOUT BARRIERS

"For God so loved the world that He gave His only begotten Son, that whoever believes in Him should not perish, but have everlasting life."
~ John 3:16

MEDITATION

Few things are as heartbreaking as a wall built around you. Some barriers we cling too: small-mindedness, broken relationships, and sin. Our sin is a barrier that separates us from God. When God sent His only begotten Son into the world to save us from our sins, He broke the barrier through His Son's sacrificial death on the cross and His resurrection. Jesus longs for us to experience His love with no barriers. Today, you must ask the question - what barriers are separating me from God's best things in life? Examine your heart and see if there is any condemnation, filter out the old and contrary way of life, come to Jesus, just as you are and

He will make you brand new, try Him, He is so wonderful, loving and forgiving and you can remain with Him throughout eternity.

PRAYER

Dear Lord, stir my heart and remove the barriers that keep me from loving You and spending time with You. Your Name brings peace, hope, and joy to my soul. Lord, I need thee every hour, every hour I need thee, I thank You and give Your Name the glory, In Jesus' name. Amen.

THE SOLID ROCK

"Jesus Christ is the chief cornerstone."
~ Ephesians 2:20

MEDITATION

The Bible refers to Jesus as a Rock who never changes. I can testify that He is the SOLID ROCK on which we can build our lives. My hope is built on Jesus blood and righteousness. I dare not trust the sweetest frame, but holy lean on Jesus Name. When the storms of life beat against us, while we do not look at the things we can see, for the things we can see are temporary, but the things we cannot see are eternal. Jesus is our precious cornerstone. Put all your trust in Him, become totally dependent on the SOLID ROCK. Let the church say Amen.

PRAYER

Dear Lord, thank You for reminding us that we can stand on the name of Jesus, our Solid Rock. When the storms of life are raging, I will call on the name of Jesus. When I am sad, I will call on the name of Jesus. Christ, the ROCK, our hope, peace, and joy. Amen.

RELATIONSHIP WITH GOD

"Jesus said unto them, I am the way, the truth and the life, no man cometh unto the Father, except by me."
~ John 14:6

MEDITATION

Building an earthly relationship is sometimes difficult, it can become taxing. A healthy earthly relationship requires diligence, communication, patience, trust, and time. A relationship with God is no exception. Building a relationship with God will require spending time in His Word, praying, listening, and talking to Him. Allow God to speak to you, as you study His Word, take time to linger in His Word and ask Him for understanding. As you spend time with God, your life with Him will deepen. You will find that the results are well worth the effort and "He is a friend who loves you all the time, and

He is a rewarder to those who diligently seek Him." His word will empower your life and you will be a blessing to others. Hallelujah

PRAYER

Dear Lord, thank You for reminding me that I need to spend time with You every day. Help me to build a closer relationship with You through Your Word and prayer. Lord, I need thee every hour. In Jesus' name. Amen.

HOPE & EXPECTATION

"Now faith is the substance of things hoped for, the evidence of things not seen."
~ Hebrews 11: 1

MEDITATION

I praise God for the revelation of HOPE and EXPECTATION, these two travel together. As believers, we must never lose HOPE because God has promised us peace, joy, and eternal life. Let us face each day with trust in our God. Let us teach our children and love ones to do the same. I am in my golden years now and I wake up each morning with HOPE and EXPECTATION from my Father in heaven. His promises are sure, and His Word will not return unto Him void - Hallelujah! Begin to HOPE and EXPECT again, God is a PROMISE KEEPER!

PRAYER

Dear Father, when my heart is troubled, let me trust in YOU. When I become discouraged, let me depend upon YOU. When I lose faith in this world, let me hold tightly to my faith in YOU. Remind me, Lord that in every situation and in every season of my life, YOU will love me, and protect me. Lord, thank YOU that You are my strength and I need thee every hour. In Jesus' name. Amen.

SEEING OTHERS

"Trust in the living God."
~ 1 Timothy4:10

MEDITATION

Seeing others through the eyes of God can be very difficult. The single reason: we live in our small environments and we think of others being less than we are, let's get over ourselves, "For God so loved the world, that He gave His only begotten Son, that whosoever believes in Him should not perish, but have everlasting life" (John 3:16). As we mature in God's Word and His love, we will begin to see others with love, forgiveness, patience, and gentleness. Jesus left this instruction with His disciples, "a new commandment I give unto you. That you love one another as I have loved you (John 13:34)." A believer must be that light that shines bright in the home, community, church, school, and workplace. Trust in the living God to help you SEE OTHERS through His eyes. You will begin to function differently, you will smile more, and you will love others unconditionally. As mature fathers and mothers, when we correct the younger men and women, we will do so with love and kindness. Let's teach our children that everyone is important in God's eyes. God's ways and thoughts are higher than ours, and believers should be maturing every day. Hallelujah!

PRAYER

Dear Lord, forgive me for my selfish sins. Help me Lord to see others through Your eyes of love. Today, let forgiveness rule my heart. Lord, let my love for Christ be reflected in those who cross my path every day. I thank You and give Your Name glory and honor. In Jesus' name Amen

ENCOURAGEMENT

"Feed the flock of God which is among you."
~ 1 Peter 5:2

MEDITATION

I am learning to think and pause before I speak. I am learning not to address every little circumstance that comes my way. Oh, what a blessing in my life. This decision comes from years of making mistakes, praying, and studying His Word. Today, I seek to encourage the next generation and I am less stressful in the process. Begin to measure your words carefully, speak wisely, and not impulsively. Our verse today: Feed the flock which is among you, not with hateful and means words, but with gentleness and love. Our words can encourage someone or offend someone. Words do hurt! Be a blessing every day and encourage someone. The harvest is truly great, but the labors are few.

PRAYER

Dear Lord, I thank You for Your grace and mercy. Thank You for dying on the cross to save me. Today, let me help my family and others find the strength and the courage to bless others with kind words and actions. In Jesus' name. Amen.

DECEIVED

"And Jesus answered and said to them, take heed that no one deceives you."
~ Matthew 24:4

MEDITATION

I thank God for His many blessings in my life and my family's life. Today, we live in a world where DECEPTION is embracing our people at an alarming rate. TRUTH is pushed aside as people create their view of the Bible and their own moral system of beliefs. As children of God, we must pray for discernment as we navigate through this life. Your life may be the only Bible someone may read today. Our pastor reminds us to keep God's Word front and center in our lives with our spiritual armor firmly in place. The Holy Bible is our road map to heaven. Take heed that no one DECEIVES you with untruths, half-truths, and vain beliefs.

PRAYER

Dear Lord, thank You for reminding me of Satan's deceptive ways. I thank You that Your Word is TRUTH. Give me wisdom and understanding that I may be a blessing to others. As I share the good news of Your saving power. In Jesus' name. Amen.

FORGIVENESS

"Blessed are the merciful, for they will be shown mercy."
~Matthew 5:7

MEDITATION

The night of June 17, 2015 (the Emanuel 9 tragedy) left me wrestling with forgiveness. God's Word is clear on FORGIVENESS, we must forgive those who have injured us. We must also ask others to forgive us when we have wronged them. If there exists even one person whom you have not forgiven (and that includes yourself), follow God's commandment and His will for your life: FORGIVE. Sometimes, we must avoid the company of others who always bicker and complain about every little circumstance. Forgiveness is not an emotion, forgiveness is an act of LOVE. Jesus' death on the cross was about forgiveness.

PRAYER

Dear Lord, forgiveness is Your Commandment, and I will admit that sometimes FORGIVENESS is difficult. Help me to forgive those who have injured others and me. Lord, deliver me from the traps of others who hold onto bitterness and un-forgiveness. I know that FORGIVENESS is Your way and I want to live according to Your commandments. In Jesus' name. Amen.

PARENTS

"Except the Lord builds the house we labor in vain".
~ Psalm 127:1

MEDITATION

Raising a family is not easy. I am the mother of two sons and one daughter, grandmother of seven, I am blessed to be the neighborhood mother and adopted mother and grandmother of a few. I am so grateful to God for my family. Parents want the best for their family, take time every day to seek God on behalf of your family. Proverbs 22:6 is our guide: "Train up a child in the way he should go and when he is old, he will not depart." Children are like arrows, we must point them in the right direction.

Teaching your child(ren) the Lord's Prayer, Ten Commandments, and the 23rd Psalm will bless and empower them throughout their life. God is a Promise Keeper.

PRAYER

Dear Lord, thank You for my family. Let me seek You every day on behalf of my biological, church, community, and work families. Help me to be courageous in speaking truth to them, and praising them along the journey. Thank You, Lord for the gift of family. In Jesus' name. Amen.

GENEROSITY

"He that hath two coats, let him impart to him that hath none, and he that hath meat, let him do likewise."
~Luke 3:11

MEDITATION

Families, neighbors, and friends continue to recover from the South Carolina Flood of 2015. The Bible is clear with instructions on how believers should response to those in need. I give a shout-out to all families, churches, communities, agencies, individuals, and our leaders who have blessed others with their time, talent, and treasure. Proverbs 11:25: He who has a generous heart, will receive a generous blessing. A quote from the late Dr. Martin Luther King, Jr: "everybody can be great, because anybody can serve." There is need all around you, open your heart to those in need and give your love, time, talent and treasure. The act of kindness will bless you!

PRAYER

Dear Lord, You have been generous with me, let me continue to be generous with others. Help me to be generous with my time, my treasure, and my possessions as I care for others. As South Carolina recovers from the loss of loved ones, homes and businesses, give me patience each day as I face small inconveniences. Lord, I ask You to keep me humble, and give me boldness to share the Love of Jesus with someone who needs to feel your presence. Lord, we give glory and honor to Your Name. Amen.

YOUR INFLUENCE

Clothe yourself with compassion, kindness, humility,
gentleness and patience.
~ Colossians 3:12

MEDITATION

God has entrusted each of us with influence in the lives
of others. We have an awesome responsibility in
friendships, spouses, children, co-workers, and friends
to share the good news of Jesus. For this reason,
followers of Christ are urged and encouraged to be
patient and gentle with one another. Parents do not
press too hard or demand too much from your children
all the time. Let your light so shine before your
children, seek God and pray on your children's behalf.
We can trust God in every circumstance and situation.
He is all wise and all-knowing and He loves you.

PRAYER

Dear Father, thank You for reminding me of your unconditional love for humanity. Lord, help me to be a good influence to my family, church, neighbors, friends and those I meet on my journey. What You did for us on Calvary's cross to save us from our sins, let us go forth and be clothe with compassion, kindness, humility, gentleness and patience as we share the good news of Your saving power. In Jesus' Name. Amen.

GOD'S TIMING

"The steps of the Godly are directed by the Lord. He delights in every detail of their lives."
~ Psalm 37:23

MEDITATION

From birth and throughout our life, we are impatient creatures. We know what we want and we want it NOW! God has created a world that unfolds according to His own timetable, not ours. When we read about biblical leaders, for example Abraham and Sarah, we see it was not uncommon for God to ask His people to wait. Not just a day or two, but to wait years. Waiting has taught me P-A-T-I-E-N-C-E, a virtue I needed for this journey in life. While you are waiting on God, spend time with the Father in prayer, study and meditate on His Word, attend Bible Study on a regular schedule. The more time we spend with the Father and know His promises, we become empowered and we can be a blessing to the masses waiting to hear about our Loving Savior.

PRAYER

Dear Lord, You have a plan for my life, and Your timing is always right for me. When I am impatient, remind me that You are never early or late. You are always on time. I trust You, and I thank You Lord. In Jesus' name. Amen.

DELIVERANCE

"Is anything too hard for the Lord?"
~ Genesis 18: 14

MEDITATION

God knows our frame, He is mindful of our limited understanding and limited faith. Because of our limitations, we place limitations on God. As you seek God and His wonder working power in your life, begin to trust His plan for your life. A few years ago, my family witness God's blessings and deliverance. My six year old grandson became ill at school, he was admitted to the hospital, six days went by and the doctors had no answer for us and my grandson became worse. When you cannot feel God's presence, You can trust His promises. Early Sunday morning, my son called from the hospital with good news, the doctors found the cause of his illness and medicine would cure his illness. Thanks be to God for is wonder working power. God worked through the doctors and staff to heal my grandson. Put your trust in Him every day and begin to experience His endless love, deliverance and awesome power.

PRAYER

Heavenly Father, Your infinite power is beyond my human understanding. Lord, with You, nothing is impossible to me. I ask that You keep me mindful of Your power in my life every day. May I remember Your goodness and mercy down through the years. Lord, let me expect the miraculous when I trust in You. In Jesus' name. Amen.

MISTAKES

"He who conceals his sins does not prosper, but whoever confesses and renounces them finds mercy."
~Proverbs 28:13

MEDITATION

As adults and believers, we are far from perfect. And, without question, our children and grandchildren are imperfect. However, when we make mistakes, we must correct them and ask forgiveness. When our children and grand-children make mistakes, let us teach them the same kindness and mercy that Jesus shows us. If there is some unforgiveness in your heart with family, friends, or others that you have been struggling with, cast all your cares on Him. He cares for you and wants you to rest in Him. Read 1 Peter 5:7. We are the apple of His eye. Amen

PRAYER

Heavenly Father, I am imperfect and I fail You in many ways. Thank You for your forgiveness and unconditional love. When others fall short of Your commandments, Lord, let me forgive them and love them. Thank You for Your great mercy each day. In Jesus' name. Amen.

POSSESSIONS

"Whoever loves money never has money enough, whoever loves wealth is never satisfied with his income."
~ Ecclesiastes. 5:10

MEDITATION

We grow up, get an education, raise our family, work, and retire the first 60 or 70 years of our life. Since the South Carolina Flood, I have met people who have so much possessions they are wondering what to do with it. We all need basic essentials in life, but once those needs are met for ourselves and our families, we should ask God to help us to share with others. I have begun to clean out closets and give away some of my possessions. Our real riches are not of this world. Everything has a season in this life. As I enjoy the latter days of this earthly life, I am learning to let go of so much stuff, I am slowing down and enjoying a nice conversation with others including my family. If you find yourself running all the time, take inventory of your life; what we often possess, often possess us. Stop and smell the roses, this may be your season to enjoy the roses. Let the church say Amen!

PRAYER

Dear Lord, keep me mindful that my riches are found in You. Deliver me from greed and let me share my possessions, both material and spiritual with those in need as often as I can. Let me be a humble and cheerful giver, and I thank You for the many blessings you have bestowed upon me. Amen.

PRAYER

"Watch ye therefore and pray always."
~ Luke 21:36

MEDITATION

PRAYER is as essential to the believer as food is to the body. PRAYER changes things and it changes us. Jesus gave His disciples the Model Prayer.

There are four components to my prayer: (1) adoration (2) confession (3) thanksgiving and (4) petitions.

Our Father which art in heaven, hallowed be thy name thy kingdom come, thy will be done in earth, as it is in heaven. Give us this day our daily bread and forgive us our debts, as we forgive our debtors. And lead not into temptation, but deliver from evil. For thine is the kingdom, and power and the glory, forever Amen.

Find time each day to pray and seek God. Prayer will empower you for the mission God has ordained for your life.

PRAYER

Pray the *Our Father's...* prayer. May God bless you to attend a church of your choice, and may the Lord bless you real good!

GOD IN THE STORM

"He is excellent in Power."
~ Job 37:23

MEDITATION

Reading and studying the Book of Job reminds us as humans how feeble we are in this journey of life. We are unable to understand why small children lose their lives tragically, church and family members are taken away suddenly, and why injustice in the system does not work for the good of all people. God's Word declares, "We are like dust, but His grace is sufficient for you and my strength is made perfect in your weakness." (2 Corinthians 12:9). We can trust an all-wise and all-knowing God in the storm. Job's trust in God made his latter days better than his beginning days. Please read and study the Book of Job. Hallelujah to His Holy Name.

PRAYER

Dear Lord, I sing because I am happy. I sing because I am free, I sing because I trust You to keep me in the storm. Thank You for Your unconditional love every day and thank You for blessing my family. In Jesus' name. Amen.

HEALTHY HEART

*"Keep your heart with all diligence, for out of it
spring the issues of life."*
~ Proverbs 4:23

MEDITATION

Wearing the right fashions and keeping ourselves
looking young on the outside are popular trends for our
society. However, these trends have little importance if
our hearts harbor greed, hatred, arrogance, self-
promotion, and foolishness. How healthy is your heart?
The ingredients of a healthy heart are joy, love, peace,
longsuffering, gentleness, meekness, and faith
(Galatians 5:22). With these ingredients add grace,
mercy and compassion, you'll surely reflect a heart for
God and be a blessing to others.

PRAYER

Dear Lord, teach me to value my heart more than I value the externals. Grant me wisdom to cultivate the internal ingredients that will make my heart healthy for my journey. Thank You for keeping my mind stayed on You, and may I be a blessing to others every day. In Jesus' name. Amen.

THE BLESSING OF GIVING

"It is more blessed to give than to receive."
~ Acts 20:35

MEDITATION

The widow woman in the Bible (Mark 12:38-44) gave her last coins to support the ministry and Jesus recognized her as giving from her heart. Two thousand years have passed since this story was recorded in the Bible. But, thanks be to God, He is the same yesterday, today and forever. God's faithful promises to His children are the same; He is true to His Word. His Word declares, *It is more blessed to give than to receive.* The act of giving reminds us that we live by God's grace. Decide today, to give the ten percent of your time, talent, and treasure required from God to your church. The Bible also instructs us to give an offering to assist others. Giving also expresses our confidence in God that He will supply all our needs according to His riches in glory.

PRAYER

Dear Lord, please help me to trust You in all areas of my life. Thank You Lord for sending Your beloved Son to die for my sins and that I can trust You to provide for all my needs. Remind me often – It is more blessed to give than to receive. In Jesus' name. Amen.

A Note from the Author

You can be sure of your salvation:

Jesus said to him, I am the way, the truth, and the life. No one comes to the Father except through me.

John 15:6

■■

If you confess with your mouth the Lord Jesus and believe in your heart that God has raised Him from the dead, you will be saved. Romans 10:9

■■

Sinner's Prayer:

Dear Lord, I confess that I am a sinner. I believe that Jesus died on the cross for my sins, the third day, He arose from the dead. Jesus, I want you come into my heart and save me. Amen.

_____

Name

_____

Date of your salvation

God bless you!

Made in the USA
Columbia, SC
15 October 2021